Song of the Constant Sea

Also by Richard Owens

Poetry
Delaware Memoranda (Blazevox 2008)
Embankments / Outtakes / Uppercuts (Blazevox 2010)
Ballads, 1st Edition (Habenicht Press 2012)
No Class (Barque Press 2012)
Ballads, 2nd Edition (Eth Press 2015)
Poems (Blazevox 2019)

Criticism
Sauvage: Essays on Anglophone Poetry (Blazevox 2019)

Song of the Constant Sea

Richard Owens

Shearsman Books

First published in the United Kingdom in 2021 by
Shearsman Books Ltd
PO Box 4239
Swindon
SN3 9FN

Shearsman Books Ltd Registered Office
30–31 St. James Place, Mangotsfield, Bristol BS16 9JB
(this address not for correspondence)

www.shearsman.com

ISBN 978-1-84861-791-9

For our Little C

Finding home where home is not—what
exile utterly shreds the chest—what remains
of the womb—these last vestiges of sound
and stone that smack of an old familiarity.

Ancient is a word. It tells us that we were
not the first—not by a long shot—not when
migration drags us like iron shavings
across the surface of a sphere too many
poets caught the movement of—and the sea
was never me—was never mine—but the
rivers that drain into it and the mountains
that flank them so flagrantly—these belonged
to mine—ours—the Delaware curling down
from Hancock—the nexus where Pennsylvania
—place my Father was born and New York
where he worked and New Jersey where my
Mother traces her people back to the farmland
along the banks—Bloomfield—landed
gentry and when the land went bad they took
their name to the factories just to feed themselves.

What could such place be to we. Old familiarity
—that of a stranger—estrangement—a woe
and discomfiture unsuited to such a fragile set
of bone and flesh—the mind as much a part
of all that as the foot or knee that listens as do
the ears—and under what stars do we see
our sign when influence was according to the
ancients an ethereal fluid that flowed forth
from the stars and each according to their lights.
The sea is not for we. Simply put. But I stand
as witness to it—the lobstermen here in Maine
—in Harpswell—that village when it takes
a village to raise an idiot like me when way back
we imagined the world in its worlding when
we said the whole of this Earth is a global village.

On the Devil's Back Trail in Harpswell
I watched with my family seals upon a rock at
the center of Long Cove—a stone between one
shore and another—the water salt not fresh like
my Mother said we were when we told lewd
jokes that made her blush—but that was in Jersey
—not far from the banks of the Delaware where
my Brothers and I swung off a rope and into
the river at a stretch of bank inhabited by Colonel
Hairtrim who lived in an old camper just off
the Old Mine Road where somewhat recently my
Father and I stood in total awe at the final
resting place of a veteran of the Indian Wars
—the remains of a cemetery stitched to what once
was the Minisink Church and no longer stands
which is how history and exile and home do work
or at least that is the labor they perform as when
in Amazing Grace they say the Earth shall dissolve
like snow—and tonight here in Scarborough
it snows on this day—23 March 2020—and the
plow trucks rumble up and down the road scraping
the asphalt and throwing sparks into the weather.

Mike Basinski used to tell me the only thing
Jonathan Williams ever cared to talk about was
the weather—and even when I spoke with him
back in 2007 all he talked about was the weather
and that was in June and he said everything was
lush—and he had the photographer Reuben Cox
out behind the house on Scaly Mountain
at Skywinding Farms—Highland—North Carolina
—he had Reuben Cox pulling weeds and there
was a tall weed I pulled from the ground that day
my Father and I drove wildly up the badly asphalted
Old Mine Road—a road built along an old Native
American foot trail that went back centuries if not
millennia—and that weed—which I just caught

out of the corner of my eye as we rumbled past it
was Common Mullein which I capitalize here
if only because it was and is a staple ingredient in
North American Native American knik-knik—the
miscellaneous herbs Native Americans blended
with their tobacco—and we—US Americans—
regard the plant as a weed but it has overwhelming
healing properties—the respiratory system in
particular—to offset the harm of smoking as such
and I wondered then and I wonder now why
after I pulled that weed and dried it and smoked
it—I wondered why American physicians—all of
whom took the Hippocratic Oath—I wondered
why American physicians who swore to do no harm
would send us to the horror of pharmacies rather
than send us to supermarkets or into the woods.
Steve Jobs—the creator of the touch screen—used to
say: If food is not your medicine then medicine
will be your food. But our doctors fed us heroin
and we lost friends and we lost family members and
the doctors still send us to pharmacies rather than
supermarkets and forests—and they do terrible harm
slicing us open and stuffing us with hyper-processed
pills when many Native American communities
were capable of healing cancer with song and dance
and what the forests offer gladly as gifts. We
are slow to learn—but the Old Mine Road teaches
and it taught me that day just a year or so ago when
I traveled it with my Father as Fathers often do.
Jonathan Williams traveled through the forests of
North Carolina with Reuben Cox photographing the
remains of log cabins built by Joe Webb—a master
of the art. My Father lives in a cabin he and my
Brother and some friends built with their bare hands
after a crew came up to Jersey from Tennessee
and assembled the hand-hewn logs like Lincoln Logs.

The home I write in does and does not belong to us
and in the end it will always be a home we can
never hope to own—like the song from that London
pub rock band the Jook—but here we are—living
—for now—this little home with a history all
its own—brought here from New Hampshire around
1910 by the fiddle maker Lewis Litchfield who
we were told carried luggage as a child for Henry
Wadsworth Longfellow—who made and played
fiddles through to mid-century as he worked the ticket
office for the Maine-New Hampshire line—and
the *Christian Science Monitor* reports this but we had
no clue who owned this place when we first arrived.
All we knew was that we found a house on the cheap
back in 2010—but the place was completely
uninhabitable and so we hired this contractor who was
related to some judge in Chicago and he took us for
everything we had and did not a lick of work
on the place—and I remember the night we arrived
with our child who was then just on the
other side of a year old—and I watched my Wife
collapse into weeping while I howled and thrashed
and my child crawled around in filth—no
toilet—no shower—no room not expressly defined
by filth—and so we pulled ourselves together
and my Father and my Twin Brother and I—we
threw ourselves into work—hosing ourselves
off on a sheet of plywood in the backyard when
we needed to bathe the grime from our flesh and we
made the place habitable—but not before my
Brother lost his job as a construction worker for
staying to help rather than reporting to work—and we
did this and we lived this as people live in the world.

Building home where home is not. This is not always
a choice—nor is it necessity in the philosophical sense.
Let me speak plainly—poetically. Helen Nearing

says there is no religion higher than truth. Scott Nearing
says pay as you go. Do not allow the economy to
make a bid on your future. Do not allow yourself to be
enslaved by what severs your relation to this world.

Out behind the house—among the life teeming over
no different than an overwhelmed sea slamming
the fluidity of its disgruntled body against the rocks
—are friends I scarcely thought I could count
among those I love—Horse Chestnut and Nettle and
Wild Blueberry and Raspberry and Reeds and
Birches and Oaks and Maples and the many varied
Pines and Spearmint growing up from the ground
—all no less wild than I might be on a drunk on
any night the Good Lord might grant—and when
the wind whistles the pines whisper—Spruce and
Cedar and what my mother used to call the
Scotch pines—their long needles like the quills of
a porcupine and my Father told me the Blackfoot
were a prideful people—their hair—their hair they
would grow out as long as 10 feet and wash it
daily in rivers and streams and comb bear grease
through it using the tail of a porcupine and so the
needles of the Scotch pine strike me as I gaze
on the medley of dry leaves beneath my feet—the
Maple and the Oak and the Birch—and the beds
of needles I might walk upon barefoot and never
fear for comfort—but here we look toward the
Penobscot and the Wabanaki and the Passamaquody
and the Mi'kmaq who drive the same Ford
and Chevrolet and GMC trucks my neighbors do
—and when I see these Leviathan critters
driving beside me on the interstate—these massive
utility vehicles driven by workers that would
sell their souls to command these vehicles and then
massive grills like tusks or teeth and the robust
metallic bulk of their front ends—their squat beds

and their majestic height—these trucks—trucks—
trucks—when I drive beside them on the
interstate I believe I run with the buffalo as in the
days of old—their metallic hoods glistening
like the brows of bison in the midday sun and it is
hard to let them go—to break from the running
herds and I hear the voices of a thousand ancient
trees whispering and the rubber hooves of the herds
stampeding over the rumble strips on the asphalt.

But the buffalo were always already more than this
and I remember sitting with Brother Anthony
and Kim Kwang-Kyu on the banks of Lake Erie when
my Love and I showed them around Buffalo and
Kim Kwang-Kyu stood heavy on the banks thinking
and he said to us—he said to us—slowly and
deliberately he said Erie—ee-ri—is Korean for wolf
and there was something of the wolf inside him
though not as we might understand it because all we
ever see is predatory violence in these creatures
—but no—it was not this—it was another aspect of
the creature Kim Kwang-Kyu identified with
—something of the noble aura concealed deep in
snow-covered forests—their manes like those
of lions—and white as the snow—and quiet—and
there is something of the buffalo I feel when
I think through my lines and look into the face of
my child and then into the face of my Father
and so on down the line—such massive creatures
with the strength of Herakles or Samson and
without the impulse to hurt or kill so much as a fly
and how as they saunter across the plains
they merely swat the flies that swarm them with
their tails and move on to the grasses that
might interest them—deliberately—slowly—with
out concern for anything beyond what their

attentions are fixed upon—their rolling backs
like the workers in my family—slow—deliberate.

Saint Paul says clearly in *Corinthians* we see now
only in part—but later we will see all—just as now
we grasp only in lyric and yet epic is promised us
—when we have been true—unto ourselves
and those we love. There was a day when my family
and I were in Buffalo—the place I did graduate work
—and we went to Buffalo Rome—and roam
Buffalo do—and after we went to the Church of
the Holy Angels—an Episcopalian chapel and this
denomination being clearly closest to my own
Catholicism—and a week earlier I had confessed
and so with my beloved Wife and with
my child I received the host—this substantiation
and I had not been denied by God—and my
longing was answered by the Holy Spirit precious
in my heart just as Saint Augustine says: God is
a circle whose circumference is nowhere and whose
center is everywhere—always already at once I
believe—and what solace this has been to me when
every particle that exists is precious and sacred:
every shining pine needle; every hair on every head.

And the Buffalo that roamed across this continent
were slaughtered to extinction just as Chief
Seattle said: I saw a thousand rotting Buffalo
slain across the plains—shot from the windows
of passing trains—those iron horses on steel tracks
and now the only bison left are bred as meat
when on the walls of ancient caves in northern Spain
and southern France and out in Sumatra are buffalo
inscribed on the walls of caves by ancient hands
and so I look to my Little Buffalo—my Iron Mensch
—my child—to steadily carry the weight of this living
into the future like a herd a thousand strong raging

into the living that must be done with deliberation and
steady hands and a heartfelt mind and intelligent heart.

Then there are friends—each with an aura and spirit
specific to the lights that shine from their eyes—
ole Kent Johnson fly fishing the creeks and streams of
Illinois and Wisconsin—casting and reeling again.
Olson said fishing is a holy calling—voca—this voice.

They will know us by what we leave behind—refuse
—trash and resistance—what stubbornly remains.
The letters distant from the larynx are what befuddle us.

There is a gap—as when I see the bodies on the street
and search for the appropriate pronoun when
mensch I am told is gender neutral—and so—the man
or the woman or the being my eyes fall upon rise up
to meet eyes that exceed the limits of what language
can offer and I remain gripped by the difficulty of it all
when I imagine we are plural—each of us—in ways
my hands tear at stone in order to simply understand.
Saint Augustine says God is a circle Whose
Circumference is nowhere and Whose Center is
Everywhere. Hegel says the Spirit is a Bone.
These are the same statement. This is beyond dispute.

Ethnos. We have forgotten the true origin of nation.
There are the lines—straight—curved—broken—
coiled round one another—bent and twisted and braided.
We forgot that the word nation was code for community
or what we Marxists might call a social formation.
Ethnos comes from the ancient Greek but was taken up
by the Romans which is where the nic comes in.

But—O—my Little One—let me speak to you—this
way with these words and I will tell you My Precious
how your Great Grandmother—my Nanny Owens—

trained as a nurse—to heal the ill—how each and every
Owens that served in the military served always in
the Medical Corp—and how your Father when I did not
have to work in factories or shops served the poor
and the ill and the disabled and the infirm—how I took
the same oath any medical doctor might—the one
Hippocrates gave us—DO NO HARM—and let me tell
you how I took this oath as a Medic in the US Army
and how my Great Uncle Davie Owens who was also
a medic died in a car crash and how your Great
Grandfather—my Pop Pop Ward—was a medic who
served in the South Pacific during WWII and received a
Purple Heart for tending to the wounded under fire
on a beach on a South Pacific island and how your Father
has served with joy Migrant Farmworkers and the ill
and infirm and how I lifted with joy the bodies of
the disabled—the intellectually and physically disabled
—and how so much more intelligent they were than
me and how much they taught me—and how I wiped
away the waste from their bodies and freshened their
garments so they could teach me more so that I could
learn what it means to be here in this place on this Earth
and how God allowed me to serve the homeless
most of whom are mentally ill like me and how they
teach me what it means to be here in this place on this Earth.

But let me tell you also of Maundy Thursday—when we
should wash the feet of others—when I was in Korea
where your Mother was born in dire poverty I was
in the Army working at a small medical clinic tending to
the ill and the infirm—let me tell you how I watched
a doctor—a Captain—who took the same oath I did before
God—how I watched him allow an indigent woman
desperate for love wash his feet when he should have been
washing hers—and he degraded her—right before my eyes
and he looked to me with his eyes and spoke gleefully
of how this woman bent over his body to wash his feet when

he should have been washing hers—and O my Little One
I wept and I wept and I wept as I so often do because there
are injustices that cannot be registered under the laws we
are forced to live by but—O—my Little One there is always
a higher authority to answer to and there always will be
though the religion called science would have us all believe
otherwise and so please if only for your sake—and the
sake of your soul—accept none of it—and weep always
for those who suffer because your tears will cleanse
your soul and you will be renewed and you will be
fortified so that you can tend to who and what you
must as a responsible citizen living on the face of
this Earth—and do not allow those practitioners of
the religion called science to tell you that the art of healing
is reducible to cutting us open and stuffing us with
pills because if you stay in one place for just a little
while and keep shitting into the Earth in that place
the Earth itself will grow the things that will heal you
just as not far from where our waste falls into
the Earth we have seen Nettle grow—and that my
Little One is one of the few plants that most cancer
foundations agree can both treat and prevent cancer
and so if I had known this back when the great poet
Edward Dorn—the architect of the Gunslinger—had
cancer I would have told him not to write CHEMO
SABE but instead I would have told him to forgo
the radiation and drown himself in Nettle—but instead
of Nettle needles they stuck him with metal needles
that sapped not only his energy but also the whole of his
spirit when Native Americans were known to heal
cancer simply by singing to one and another with love
but as the great poet Robert Duncan said in order
for this to be we must BELIEVE BELIEVE BELIEVE.

Plato kicked the poets out of the Republic because he
did not—was not allowed to—know God and this is
because he betrayed Socrates by writing down his words

and it is the poets—according to the dialog Ion—that
are allowed to know God—allowed to sing with all the
Angels and Saints in Heaven—with the spirits that guide
us—and if we listen to the Angels—these envoys of God
then we cannot function among those who would tear
at the Earth and murder and enslave and we cannot
listen to the practitioners of the religion called science
who would have us sliced open and stuffed with pills
when simple and beautiful things like Wheat Bran
in Europe and Alum in the Americas have been used
as effective remedies for many varieties of mental
illness which is really just a temporary stage in a process
that should be regarded as a blessing and not a curse.
The Catholic Church calls poets Cantors—like the Cantos.
So what I mean to say is this: Live with the total Fury of
your Whole Heart and heal and aid those you can as you can
and weep when you must because it is this that will teach
and not the vain fashions that pass like an ephemeral breeze
through the universities and libraries and hospitals and halls.

And here we reside—in a small home built by Lewis
Litchfield who used to carry luggage for Henry Wadsworth
Longfellow—and it was no library or university that
introduced me to the first poem Longfellow wrote at the
age of 13—it was my Father who while I sat on the front
porch smoking just off Ridge Road—which was the name
of the same road William Carlos Williams lived on down
in Rutherford—but we were in Montague—New Jersey—
near the Delaware River where I swam as a child and my
Father excitedly brought over a copy of his *Muzzleloader*
magazine which he got at the Shop-Rite at the end of
River Road—and he showed me an article on the ranger
Captain John Lovewell who fought against Abenaki Chief
Paugus up here in Maine—at the bend of the Saco River
which is the river from which we draw our precious
drinking water and the water we bathe in—and the poem
Longfellow first published—"The Battle of Lovewell's

Pond"—talks about the "savage's yell" when in
French the word savauge simply means close to the Earth
and at this bend in the Saco River near Fryeburg here in
Maine it was the Pigwacket (Pequawket) who were
provoked by settlers and they were members of the larger
Sokokis community of whom Chief Squandro was
leader and the son of Squandro who as a toddler was
thrown into the Saco River by European settlers who
wanted to see if the Native American child could swim
instinctively like dogs do and the child drowned and
Chief Squandro cursed the Saco River so that each and
every year after his son was murdered by settlers
people of European extraction would drown each year
in that river—and every year since at least three people
are taken by the river—but then there was Father Rasle who
fought against the English alongside the Abenaki speaking
peoples—Rasle or Rale a Jesuit priest aiding the Native
Americans who were attacked by forces led by the English
military officer Captain Jeremiah Moulton and to this
day members of the Moulton family work in law enforcement
—the chief of police here in Scarboro a man by the name
of Moulton who has martialed considerable resources
in fighting against the opioid crisis and how it has devastated
our communities—our families—our neighbors—our
loved ones—but Lovewell's Pond is also known as
Saco Pond and Thoreau and Hawthorne too wrote about the
same battle that Longfellow wrote about at the age of 13
and each Christmastide you know we go to the Longfellow
monument on Congress Street in Portland to see if the
figure of Longfellow has a scarf to keep him warm
through the holiday season—but it was my Father who
gave me the issue of the drugstore magazine *Muzzleloader*
where I first read this line: "Cold, cold is the north wind…"

Now I listen to Modoc Native Americans from Northern
California speaking—interviews my Older Brother
recorded and shared with me many many years ago and

from the high desert plateau near Alturas—California—
where my Brother then lived with his family—and I hear
a Modoc woman talking about how no one eats squirrel
anymore but I remember eating squirrel after my Twin
Brother would hunt them and gut them and skin them
and wrap them in aluminum foil and stack them in the
freezer like cord wood—and he would cook them in
an iron skillet and take the cubed meat and throw it into
a stew that we all relished when we sat around the table.

But tell me—what is a sea—what is the ocean—when
we have been told by Hesiod that Okeanos was
and is a river that encircles the whole of the Earth like
a halo—when we have been told—the name of
the new contagion is Corona—when we have been told
Corona is a crown—when we have been told by
another poet named Rex if offered a crown please refuse.

The Hopi Indians speak of the Gourd of Ash—what this
Earth will be to us after we have done what we have to it
and my Great Grandfather Owens was a coal miner in
Scranton—in Wilkes Barre—where my Father just
returned from the funeral of his Uncle Billy Brock—he
married to Emma Jane Owens—and it was his Uncle
Billy Brock who showed him how to shoot a bow and
how to hunt for deer—just like Howard Hill who
wore dress just like Robin Hood and who my Father
deeply admired—and it is the name Owens that is drawn
from the Yew tree—the so-called churchyard tree—
one of which resides in every churchyard in England
guarding the spirits of the dead and carrying as Native
Americans believed our memories and our histories
and the name Owens is Welsh—Gaelic—Brythonic like
Brutus and like Arthur—and it is related like a cousin
to Eugene and to Ewan and to Evan like the middle
name of my Nephew—son of my Sister—his name
Devan Ethan Bloom—like the Bloomfield my

Mother descended from—but my Great Grandfather
was after a catastrophic mine collapse in Wilkes
Barre taken to the morgue—taken for dead—and he
awoke as perhaps many will in the Gourd of Ash—he
was I say alive and not at all dead because we do go on.

In Korea—South of the North where the mountains
rise like plumed serpents to meet the sky—we also have
family—like the Oma of your Mother who lived in a
poverty in Seoul we cannot readily comprehend—who
sold red bean curd in the shape of sacred fish on the
street to survive—whose husband was an activist who
set himself aflame in protest and died—who lived in
a single room with paper walls and raised her
daughters there—who when she was so malnourished
she could not produce enough breast milk to feed
your Mother put your Mother up for adoption—and
later she met another man she made a husband and
rose to her feet and had two other daughters—one of
whom studied English every day so she could find and
communicate with your Mother who was put up for
adoption—and the oldest daughter married a man
by the name of Yang Ok who is a preacher who has
devoted his life to ministering to the poor in Seoul
and I have seen him carry ten-pound bags of rice into
the single-room homes of deeply impoverished people
down on their luck and who have internalized the hatred
most every nation-state has for the poor—and when
your Mother and I visited he carved out time to take us
through the neighborhoods inhabited by the poorest
of the poor and there we stood in awe not only of the
work your Korean family does with the poor but
with the poor themselves who are resilient and full of
whatever piss and vinegar they might need to spit
in the face of it all and persist in the living they must do
and I remember when on the banks of the Han River
your Mother was cold in the late afternoon winds

whipping through the center of the city it was Yang Ok
who gave your Mother his coat when I did not have one
and I was grateful for what I could not provide and
it is this gratitude that I offer as an example of humility.

But then there is Easter—as today—the Seven Sorrows
of Mary which we are reminded to remember on this
day—the first a prediction—that after the birth the heart
will be pierced—then the escape to Egypt—and this
after Moses escaped with his people from Egypt—and
third the loss of the child who they later found in the
temple—asking questions as any inquisitive child might
and Mary and Joseph marveled at the mind of their
child joyously after the terror of his temporary loss fell
away—though into adulthood there was the sorrow
of witnessing the burden of the cross—that any
parent would grieve to see their child bear such a heavy
load—and then standing at the foot of the cross
knowing the crucifixion was to come—and then the
crucifixion—what a mother must bear at seeing
the death of her child—and finally the loss of the body
as such—when the child is torn away for good
and returned to the clay from which we all come and
these are the sorrows—no different than the sorrow
the wife of Oscar Alberto Martinez felt when
she saw the body of her child floating beside the body
of her husband among the reeds on the northern
shore of the Rio Grande—and would these be the
sorrows to come for the women they say have
given birth encamped and in detention on both sides
of the Rio Grande—women who reports say have
given birth in squalor—while standing—some with
their trousers still on—and how like a manger it must be
—that the birth of these children who we should
regard as our children takes place in such fetid conditions
no different than giving birth among farm animals
in a manger—and it is as such we are the children of.

God is angry—some say—and my Loving Wife says this
often—and what is sacrifice but a process toward
the total annihilation of the self so that we might see
through all the eyes around us—not our own—and this
coupled with the experience of knowing what life is
sharpens our senses to the suffering to which we must tend.

There is an artist—Adele Cohen—from Western New York
—Buffalo to be precise—who—thought she saw eternity
and did see eternity—just as John Donne did—knowing
that God is a light—that a light emanates from our divinity
—the divinity granted us and the divinity we are part of—
which sends to us as a directive the immediate need to care
for one another—not to administrate or manage bodies
but to offer the care that can be offered when care is needed
—to clean up the mess that capital leaves behind including
ourselves—and this is what others have been calling
self-care but this is not to be confused with comfort or con-
venience—just the need to care for what has been granted
us—that we are plural and work with materials that
do not belong to us—materials that must be returned to
all of what this is when the length of our days come
to an end—and so we care for what we are as we care
for others as we can—and Adele Cohen—an artist
who thought she saw eternity and did—how she was
from Western New York—and the artists she ran
among—Wes Olmsted who reproduced in his own way
the Yellow Christ like a sunrise over the horizon
and Ben Perrone who through the last few decades
stood as husband to Adele Cohen—who cared for her
art as one might care for a child and who built his own
Starry Night after Van Gogh and my Wife often says
you cannot get a Starry Night and two good ears and this
is just the way it is—that we must attend to the demands.

Around 1957 Adele Cohen studied in Buffalo with
Charles Burchfield—the great social realist—though she

turned with some ease toward Abstract Expressionism
as did many of her friends—and as many artists did she
traveled to New York City where she went to Pratt and
shared a studio somewhere down in the Village with
other artists though eventually she was derisively referred
to as "the baker's wife"—and she returned to Buffalo
though not before she met and befriended Louise Nevelson
among others—and with time she devoted herself to
an abstract and expressive art informed by her Judaism
—like Wallace Berman—like so many others we take for
granted—and how many of the Language Writers turned
back toward their faith—Susan Howe toward Calvinism
and New England Christian traditions—Hannah Wiener
toward Jewish mysticism—and none of this driven by fear
but motivated instead by awe and reverence and a clear
recognition that when true grace is bestowed we must
abide—and this is not fear or weakness but an indomitable
strength the artist would be a fool to turn away from
and cannot turn away from because once we are offered
just a glimpse of all of what this is—all of what we
have been allowed to be a part of—we cannot help but
fall to the ground—on our faces—in gratitude and
awe—and we writhe and twist and tear at ourselves for
what we have destroyed and taken so for granted—this gift
we have been entrusted with—this garden granted us to share
and to keep and to serve as the custodians of—to keep
in our custody with trust and with love and without
the avaricious belief that there is anything beyond the
actuality of always room for one more—that none
should be exiled or excluded—that we have the ability
to care for one another—to care for ourselves by
way of caring for one another—that the force of history
would simply ask that we hold one another—even
and especially as we die—for it is in the dying that our
eyes see freshly and anew what was foolishly discarded
—our trust in one another—even as we hurt one another.
And I have come to understand our Trans comrades as

anchors—as the seers between and above that keep the
rest of us grounded until at last all of us can shed
our gender assignments just as critters shed their hair
and are repeatedly renewed in the face of it all—in the
light that shines—and my Queer comrades who
underscore and outline the limits of heteronormativities
that brutalize our being when masculinity has long since
been weaponized in order to keep our muscles taught
and to keep our bodies moving and to keep our teeth
grinding and to keep our drives outrageously amped so
that we can guarantee varieties of productivity that
are misguided and so destroy the garden as we go along.

In other words—I remember how my Father marveled
when he saw Robert DeNiro—that great paragon of late
twentieth century masculinity—cross and then curl his
legs up under himself on late night television—and the
permission this gave us men to ease our clenched fists and
to allow the tension in our straining muscles to subside
but those tensions were so instrumental to the work we had
no choice but to perform—day in and day out—so that
even just putting your hands on your hips sent out a signal
that served to threaten productivity and so needed to be
policed through humor or comment or outright aggression.

Strangely somehow the first openly Gay man I ever met
was Mike Bullshit from GO!—a hardcore band from New
York that first emerged in the late 1980s but were not
included among the first wave of NYHC bands but were
instead associated with ABC-No-Rio on Rivington Street
where we used to play and see bands—and Mike Bullshit
gave us our first show at ABC with Supertouch—their
song "Searching for the Light" an adolescent staple for me
that I still play repeatedly as I would any other gospel
song—and I have this distinct recollection of Mike Bullshit
at the Pipeline on Broad Street in Newark talking over
the mic about how offensive he thought the things straight

people did in the privacy of their own homes was to him
and I remember laughing and I wonder now what life
might be like if we could just freely congregate with one
another and never have to worry about rigidly identifying
in any particular way beyond registering a commitment
to doing no harm to one another or to the one and another
the whole of this Earth is—that we are but made of what
it offers and it is of the Cosmos—and the trinkets we make
from the clay we scratch off the surface of the Earth can
never be more intelligent than the Earth as such—and what
garden would not but let us play as we please so long as
we keep from hurting one another or the garden that enables
and even the vital New Narrative writer Bruce Boone
who gave us A Century of Clouds said he wrote first for God
—for Eternity which is what Adele Cohen said she thought
she saw—and she did—but Bruce Boone said it was ambition
and careerism (vanity and ego) that make the soul go blind.

When I talk to homeless women so many talk about
 their families—the men that left them—or the men that
abused them—the children they left behind or were
disowned by or the children that have died and I have
always thought little can be worse than outliving a child
and who do we hold dear—and I remember my Father
on his hands and knees dressing and redressing daily
an open sore on the right foot of my Mother—a wound
that would not heal and persisted for years and daily
my Father would dress and redress the wound and do so
patiently—with deliberation and care—and this is love
such that it serves as an instance to me of deliberate care.

When I talk to homeless women so many talk about
their families—the men that loved them—or the men they
knew—the children they stay in touch with or who
have drifted for reasons no one can control—and I have
always thought little keeps us as grounded as those
we love—how our memories of love so often compel

the living we daily do—how even the love of
someone long gone can drive us forward into a future
we never thought possible—and I remember the
stories told me about family members and acquaintances
—how these just reside in mind as points of wonder
around which I build the actuality of the living I daily do.

And now—listening to Inuit throat singing—what
emanates from the larynx—deep down in the throat
from where such meaning is slung—the viscera of
the being of the whole body—like the sounds we make
when we sleep—when our thoughts are with God
and God alone—and yet these sounds are shared among
friends and family—when two people stand together
in the cold and hold one another by the crook of the arm
gesticulating—guttural—rhythms like the iamb—
which Pound said poets broke the back of even though it
echoed and was likely built after beating hearts in health
and what range of emotive imagining and deep history
do Inuit throat singers share with one another as they
hold each other by the arm—and what kind of medicine
is this driven by—what rhythms of being share such joy
and trauma and ancient narrative and contemporary living
and what complex systems are completely reset by song.

North American Native Americans believed the trees
hold our histories and our memories and among those
communities that fall within the Abenaki language system
there is belief in a mythical figure named Glooskap who
Joseph—a Passamaquoddy elder—inscribed in
Birch bark—and Joseph depicted Glooskap turning
man into Cedar—just as the Cedar might take up through
its roots the mineral remains of any man left on the soil
but then there is another illustration by Tomah Joseph
depicting the killing of Brother Wolf by man and I wonder
if Brother Wolf was killed because we mistook his nature.
Being raised by wolves is different than chased by wolves.

Romulus and Remus come to mind—founders of Rome.
Buffalo roam—but what does it really mean to roam—does
it mean migrate as North American Native Americans did.
Migratory patterns run like arteries through a body—full
circle—like the circulatory system—like trails left behind
or ahead depending on which season you find yourself
moving through—as in Spring when the songbirds
return to these marshes we inhabit now—and just before
sunrise I can hear the clamor of the songbirds—like
North American Native American song—but as the years
go on the clamor grows less and less intense—the song
birds fewer and fewer until at last we will have built
a terrible silence across the Earth cleansed only by fire.
The Hopi call this the Gourd of Ash—a lifelessness
en route—the trails we leave behind—migratory patterns.

Hippocrates and Galen. Greek and Roman approaches
to medicine were adapted by Medieval scholars
and balance was the lynchpin—what we might now
call homeostasis—and so the four humors—four fluids
corresponding to four temperaments—and the
interiority of the body echoing the cultural and social
and political phenomena all around us such that the
diseases that afflict us echo and reflect problems across
the external plains of our being—and so we waste away.

But let us not—let us not destroy ourselves and instead
restore ourselves like the mountain men of the
Adirondack mountains—like Noah Rondeau or George
Washington Sears who eventually adopted the
name Nessmuk from a Nipmuc Native American from
his home state of Massachusetts—Nessmuk and
Rondeau—both poets as well as mountain men who lived
as the critters do—Nessmuk who said: "To myself
I sometimes appear as a wild Indian or an old Berserker,
masquerading under the guise of a nineteenth century
American. When the straight-jacket of civilization

becomes too oppressive, I throw it off, betake myself to
savagery, and there loaf and refresh my soul." The word
savagery is indeed a curious one. In English usage
the term connotes a sense of barbarism and even cruelty
when in the French it suggests simply a closeness
to the Earth—a familiarity with our Earth rather than a
tendency toward that which would destroy what we have
and so my soul often longs for the woods—though
my soul has been sold—committed to other endeavors
and it is Nessmuk that says the one tool most essential to
navigating the North Woods is a light-weight canoe.
Among Indians—Hindi-speaking peoples—there is an
imagining of thisness or what Catholics like my
friend Michael Cross might call haecceity—the virtue
of an object or phenomenon—that which definitively
allows it to be precisely what it is—and among
the Jain worshippers of India this is referred to as
tattva—the defining virtue of an object or phenomenon.
In order to illustrate tattva Jain uses the metaphor
of a boat crossing from one bank of a river to the bank
on the other side of that river—like paying Chiron
to cross Lethe. By the time the boat crosses from one
bank to the other all is forgotten and all karmic particles
—all accumulated debts—have been shed from the soul
—the boat is emptied of all the water leaking in
through holes along the hull and the soul the boat carries
has been safely deposited after monumental struggle
and labor on the opposing river bank completely debt free.

If we take the Road to Damascus as Saint Paul did
we find that the remains of John the Baptist are
interred there. Among the Apostles it was John the
Baptist my Father favored—though my Father was
clear in telling me that most all were martyred. Saint
Jerome speaks of "white martyrdom"—a reclusiveness
or hermeticism that removes the self from civil
society such that the social formation one becomes

a part of is that of the Earth. Camel hair and locusts.
This is what John the Baptist wore and lived on
during his days in the wilderness. Susan Howe has
always been fascinated by the wilderness and often
I think of Henry David Thoreau hiking with the
Penobscot Native American Joe Polis to the peak of
Mount Katahdin here in Maine—and it was from
this peak—standing side by side with a Native inhabitant
of this place that he saw the whole world anew—the
unhandselled globe—the garden as it was in the beginning
and so it was perhaps with John the Baptist who Jerome
framed out as a "red martyr"—a figure taken for his
beliefs by violence and torture and so his head taken as
it was—but not before he baptized Jesus Christ in
the River Jordan—water from which was used to baptize
our own child—along with water from the Delaware
which my parents live along and the Saco River from
which we now get our drinking water and the Atlantic
into which all these rivers drain—all except the
Jordan River—water from which John baptized Christ.

In Cornwall—near Saint Ives—my friend the poet
John Phillips took me to an ancient Celtic well—and
I have imagined the Celtic peoples—their lines—were
founded by Aaron—Erin—Ireland—and Saint Patrick
abducted from Wales—ancient Britain—and he took all
the snakes with him though some say he chased them
away from Ireland—and Brythonic is a variety of
Gaelic—just as the Irish speak Goidelic—as do the
Scottish—but the Brythonic—from Brutus who threw
the ancient Cornish giants over the white cliffs of
Dover—or perhaps somewhere closer to Saint Michael's
Mount—one of those cliffs—and ended the hegemony
of one to begin the hegemony of another that yielded
Arthur though like Korea it is believed per a prophecy
advanced by Merlin that dragons founded Britain
before the Romans landed and Julius Caesar wrote his

Battle for Gaul—and David Jones—he writes about
that ancient Roman sculpture the Dying Gaul with his
mustache and it is in Wales they say the mustache
finds its origin—but my friend John—when I saw the
mass of his gargantuan body emerge from a tiny
European car at a train station in Cornwall I swore he
must be descended from those ancient Cornish giants.

Sea. Song of the constant sea. Constancy. Custance.
This is easy. As it should be. Unrelenting. Like the
tides—unending in their movement—like the heart—
unending in its movement—like the iamb—unending
until it is broken once and for all—this is what we
might call a heart attack which is what Charles Ives
called the unrelenting waves of psychosis he suffered.
Sea. Song of the constant sea. Constancy. Custance.
It was she that brought Christianity from Rome to the
British Isles—according to Geoffrey of Monmouth and
Chaucer and whoever else may have recorded this tale
and Saint Patrick brought it to the Gael—to Aaron Land.
Sea. Song of the constant sea. Constancy. Custance.
Arthur Custance who argued that there is a gap—and
it is this that confounds us—the space between us and
our Creator that creates havoc and possibility—the
veil or the unknown—the abyss—out of which each
and every mystery emerges—the missing link—the
space of possibility that snaps the breakers in the sea.

And if I can knock out lines like a child—merrily—do
forgive me—for I am but made of clay—no different
than the devices we build from dust scratched off
the surface of this Earth—and we would believe the
blocks we build with outstrip the intelligence of the
Earth we draw them from—and what fools are we—for
have you ever gazed on the molecular structure of clay
which was always already eminently greater than
what we build—how vines wrap round one another and

teach us how to braid how to build baskets how to live
for it is the fruit from the living vine that sustains us
and it is the living vine to which we are all nailed
and it is the living vine from which there is no escape.

Listen to the sermon Father Mapple delivers in *Moby-
Dick*. He tells the tale of Jonah—among the shortest
books in the Bible and the one Tolkien translated when
he participated in the building of the *Jerusalem Bible*
which was commissioned by Pope John Paul II—
and the great concrete poet Dom Sylvester Houédard
also worked as a translator for this endeavor but it was
Tolkien who translated the Book of Jonah from which the
whole of the sermon delivered by Father Mapple is drawn.
The whole point is that Jonah simply cannot outrun God.
There is no going off the grid. We cannot outrun our labor.
And so I work. And while working last night at
the shelter in Portland a middle-aged woman
brought out a large white sheaf of poems with the
sign of the Cross inscribed across the cover and
she asked me about two words: pandemic and
pandemonium. Perhaps one begets the other but
I could not help but focus on the prefix "pan"—
from the ancient Greek meaning all or whole or
entire or perhaps even total. Before the assassination
of Muammar Gaddafi under the Obama administration
Gaddafi—the leader of Libya—sought to create
a pan-African currency—a currency that would
allow the whole of Africa to break with European
and—perhaps most importantly—American
economic systems—to break the cycle of dependence.
Gaddafi was a revolutionary—a socialist—just
like the Kenyan economist and Father of President
Barack Obama who wanted to nationalize all
Kenyan industries in order to break unbearable cycles
of economic dependence on Europe and the US.
The horror these cycles of dependence have created

cannot be reasonably overstated. When I work
the night shift at the shelter several of the men and
women I work alongside are African immigrants
or perhaps refugees—I do not ask—though we talk
occasionally about the places they are from—
Rwanda and the Democratic Republic of Congo.
Much is just inexplicable to me—and one coworker
talks about the Rwandan genocide in such a matter-
of-fact manner that I find it difficult not to feel sorrow.
Gaddafi traced his roots back to the Bedouin peoples
or what Jesus might have properly called passers-by.
We are all passers-by—none of this is properly ours and
North American Native Americans seem to have
clearly understood this which is why most Native
American communities migrated in cycles and lived
off the land without any imagining of owning the land.
If we read the Bible closely we see that a nation is
largely a community of people and not the land to which
they are believed to be attached. Race is a strange word.
When psychiatrists talk to me they often ask if I have
"racing thoughts" and perhaps the word "diverse" might do.
The word "fleeting" works too. We could just be passers-by.

Last night there was also a woman—88—at the shelter
who asked me for a copy of the poem "Paul Revere's Ride."
Strangely that title is only the second half of the title
while the first half of the title is "The Landlord's Tale."
A landlord is a strange thing—and such a poem is a
strange thing for an elderly homeless woman to ask about.
Why did Longfellow not simply call the poem "Paul
Revere's Ride." What might it mean to be Lord of the Land
when Paul Revere served as a passer-by on the back of
a horse warning others to stand against an absentee landlord.

I wish the British were coming. Perhaps they could
bring socialized medicine with them—something
truly civic and civil like society and not a medley of

medical doctors who capitulate to the temptation
of getting wealthy or making ends meet by
peddling opioids to the working class and the working
poor—to our brothers and sisters. These doctors
took an oath—an ancient oath—a simple oath—do no
harm—and I say it too—do no harm—no harm—
because I too took this oath yet every night I see the
wreckage—the fallout—the broken bodies lumbering
around the shelter—around the streets—searching.
One if by land. Two if by sea. Seekers signal the same.

In Revere—in Massachusetts—on the way home from
my second job a few months back I stopped at a
shop called Little Oaxaca and it was there that I saw
such a rich blend of herbs and minerals—all with
deeply medicinal values—alum—a mineral that can be
used for water purification or to reconcile body odors
generated by bacteria and to treat varieties of mental
illness—marjoram which is used for both digestive and
depressive disorders—and white horehound—an herb
used as a treatment for digestive and respiratory
disorders like asthma and tuberculosis and bronchitis
and it was in Little Oaxaca—there—that I realized many
Latin Americans do approach grocery stores as
though they were pharmacies which is why Helen
Nearing spent time in Mexico studying with herbalists.

Exonomic Stimulus. What they call the CARES Act
—and perhaps this is how it rises—on the back of
a crisis—the Cronona Virus—COVID-19—a disease
that stems from our mistreatment of the animal
kingdom—the Kingdom of God—that creature we
so mistreated—the pangolin—and I once saw a pangolin
in the engine room of a boat floating down the
Mekong River between Thailand and Laos—a critter.

El Cantorito. As a Cantor—as a poet and a scholar
and an academic and an amateur philologist
my interest begins with the Word. Amiri Baraka
says the first drum was the Word. John the
Evangelist—who writes about John the Baptist
—is very clear at the start of the Gospel of
John: God is the Word. Logos. And a Canto is a can or
a cup—a vessel that holds things—like
history—like information—and this is important
because that particular word—Canto—is
derived from the Latin whereas the ancient Greek
would be Phialis which means both cup and
also to sing—just like the word Canto the word Phiale
is related to both holding things and to song
and songs hold things which is why in the ancient
oral traditions it was poetry as such that served
as holding vessels—as vessels that held vital
information just as the church Our Lady of Good
Voyage in Gloucester features images of the
Virgin Mary holding out to the world a fishing
Vessel in her hand—a Canto—a Song that holds
Vital information—and this must be attended to
because no one among us has ever truly known
what a Virgin really is in the eyes of God and
this is something we need to get right—and what
I mean to say here is quite clear: In the eyes
of God we are all Virgins—we are all pristine and
blemish free—regardless of however terribly
this world may have compromised our being in it
—regardless of how terribly this world may
have taken and destroyed the best part of us—
regardless of how sullied and filthy and unclean
this world may have left us—for in the eyes
of God we are all Virgins—each and every one of
us because as Augustine says God is a Circle
whose Circumference is Nowhere and whose Center
is Everywhere—and that means quite simply

that God inhabits each and every particle that exists
and this means quite simply that if God inhabits
each and every particle that exists then there can be
no such thing as waste and there can be no such thing
as filth and there can be no such thing as unclean
or sullied or damaged for God resides within us all
but unlike Spicer who said Poet be Like God (this
was a Golden Calf) we must instead say: Poet let us
Serve God—Poet let us serve all of what this is
to the best of our ability—let us serve all of what has
been left behind—let us serve all of what and all of
who have been degraded and disregarded—let us
regard them well—and let us record their song—let
us celebrate all of whom are not and have never
been celebrated—for this is the work we do if only
because God inhabits each and every particle that
exists and this is why we should take nothing for
granted because as that great Poet from Angleland
said there really is no free lunch—all is balance and
in the end all ledgers will be balanced and this
my friends is something we must all recognize sooner
or later—and so there is work to do—all around—
for we are all Virgins in the eyes of God and every hair
on every head is precious to God—every leaf and
every morsel of food—every critter and every insect
just as Chief Seattle maybe said in 1854: Every
Shining Pine Needle is Sacred—and so all of us in the
full plenitude of our infinite diversity must hold
one another just as a Canto properly holds song and is
a song and that song is a seal that must remain
unbroken just as the Circle remains eternally unbroken
—for this is the Song of the Constant Sea and it has
no end nor does it have beginning for in the beginning
there was the end—the Alpha and Omega—and the
first whisper was the Word—the breath that gave us
life so we could love one another and tear at one
another like jackals—by turn—by turn—just as the big

wheel turns—eternally—unbroken—everlasting—
by way of what we call Love for if God inhabits all that
exists then Our Father—Our Parent—Our Pater—
is always already apparently holding each and every one
of us each in the throes of our endless virginity and
we are as such beautiful and we are as such brilliant—as
in light—this brilliancy—that we are of the stars that
shine and we will return to them raging in dance
and raging in song just as Okeanos rages and encircles us
like a song that holds all of us for as Johan says
God is the Word and the Word is a Song and the Song
is a Circle with no Circumference whose Center
sounds through us in Celebration of the Sounding we do.